DEDICATION

To anyone and everyone.

We can all play where our feet are.

PWYFA™
PLAY WHERE YOUR FEET ARE

THE PRAYER JOURNAL

Cameron Elise Dobbs

PWYFA PLAY WHERE YOUR FEET ARE™
THE PRAYER JOURNAL

Book Two

Published by PWYFA Play Where Your Feet Are, LLC
Atlanta, GA

Hardcover ISBN: 979-8-9869148-3-1
Digital ISBN: 979-8-9869148-4-8
Audio ISBN: 979-8-9869148-5-5

Printed in the United States of America

PWYFA PLAY WHERE YOUR FEET ARE™
HOW TO LIVE A LIFE FULL OF LIVING

Book One

Copyright © 2022 by Cameron Elise Dobbs

Softcover ISBN: 979-8-9869148-0-0
Digital ISBN: 979-8-9869148-1-7
Audio ISBN: 979-8-9869148-2-4

A NOTE TO THE READER

Hi, friend!

Opening the pages of this book proves you are determined to progress toward your highest potential—and your greatest reward. Welcome to the start of a new era. Your *new era. How exciting is this!* The Prayer Journal *is the second part in a series of motivational books inspired by my first book,* PWYFA Play Where Your Feet Are™: How to Live a Life Full of Living. *Book One tells a story of pushing past perseverance, fighting against adversity, raising a hallelujah in the middle of a storm, and the ongoing pursuit of joy. If you have not read it, grab a copy to dive deep into learning and living abundantly.*

The nuts and bolts of the first book comprise this 31-day devotional that can be repeated every month as constant daily reminders, not one-time checkpoints. Together, we will walk through my favorite verses and teachings—the ones that have impacted me the most.

This book is about action. Each daily entry combines biblical truths with anecdotal experiences to help you execute "playing where your feet are." Be intentional in writing and reflecting on the questions. This journal was created to impact you. Now it's on you to change your life and the lives of those around you. Won't you join me? Let's play where our feet are!

PWYFA,
Cameron Dobbs

DAY ONE

*And I want you to know, my dear brothers and sisters, that
everything that has happened to me here has helped to spread
the Good News. For everyone here, including the whole
palace guard, knows that I am in chains because of Christ.
And because of my imprisonment, most of the believers here
have gained confidence and boldly speak God's message
without fear. . . . the message about Christ is being preached
either way, so I rejoice. And I will continue to rejoice*
(Philippians 1:12–14, 18).

Play where your feet are. These five words shaped, changed,
built, and sparked my life. Growing up, this directive from
my mother came before every practice, every tournament,
every match, and every day. It simply meant that to live a life
full of living, you must do your best and be your best, no
matter what and no matter where. Every position carries
purpose, and no role is too small for a big impact.

 Paul is the prime example of playing where your feet
are. Paul's chains were his testimony, and the position he held
—in prison, I remind you—was his platform. He fulfilled his
purpose even amidst pain. He understood his assignment and
knew no speed bump could halt progress. His purpose on
earth was to progress heaven's plan.

 Our lives are full of purpose in every position we
play. Whether you are the starter and captain or sitting left
bench, the senior or the freshman, the CEO or the youngest
intern fetching coffee, you can make an impact today.

Pick an area or two of your life. What is your current position, and how are you playing where your feet are within this season?

_____

_____

_____

_____

_____

_____

_____

_____

_____

_____

_____

_____

_____

_____

_____

_____

_____

_____

_____

_____

_____

_____

DAY TWO

We are citizens of heaven (Philippians 3:20).

I am a Georgia girl living in South Florida—an area anything but Southern. I might not be in my hometown anymore, but I still say "y'all." I still listen to country music. I still wear cowboy boots.

In our faith, we have been given certain characteristics; we have a calling that Christ has put on our lives; we have a dialect, a way we speak, and a way we live and behave. When we walk away from church on Sundays, we shouldn't lose our Christianity. Our circumstances and surroundings do not determine our identity. Our identity is not rooted in a church building, our identity is rooted in Christ. Paul didn't lose his identity outside of his home of heaven. Neither should we.

In 1 Kings 15:14 we read, "Although the pagan shrines were not removed, Asa's heart remained completely faithful to the Lord throughout his life." Our circumstances and surroundings are significant, but they shouldn't be an excuse to disobey God or downplay your purpose. People who play where their feet are can fulfill their purpose no matter the place. Location is *not* a limitation. In fact, our location should launch our role because it is within our position that our purpose is found.

Our time on earth is temporary, not trivial. Don't take up space, take advantage. Take what you have learned, the knowledge you have been taught, the sermons you have heard, and the prayers that have been prayed over you. Walk with these in every situation, playing where your feet are, no matter what and no matter where.

What is one class, group, room, or area where you can improve your efforts in playing where your feet are and impacting with intention?

_____

_____

_____

_____

_____

_____

_____

_____

_____

_____

_____

_____

_____

_____

_____

_____

_____

_____

_____

_____

DAY THREE

Many are the plans in a person's heart, but it is the Lord's purpose that prevails (Proverbs 19:21).

This verse is the biblical, more eloquent translation of the old Yiddish adage, *Mann tracht, un Gott lacht*—Man plans, and God laughs.

I had big plans growing up. As a high-caliber athlete, I planned to play ball in college, rack up several awards, then further my career in Eastern Europe. On September 7, 2019, those plans were blown to smithereens when I sustained my third brain injury within twelve months while playing volleyball for the University of Miami (UM), shattering any possibility of stepping on the court again, let alone playing professionally. Following the blow, I endured debilitating concussion symptoms for four months straight with zero improvement.

Through it all, Ephesians 3:20 became my favorite verse. God is an Ephesians 3:20 God who will do exceedingly and abundantly more than you could ever ask for. More than you could ever imagine. I never imagined becoming like a vegetable during my college junior season. I never imagined dropping out of college after being a straight-A student in the top ten percent of my class. I never imagined shifting my life's plan, but that was what was needed to follow God's plan. Turns out, He was able to do more when I had my hand in less.

Since being medically disqualified by the NCAA, I have worked as a college coach, talked with sports psychologists across the ACC, poured into thousands of athletes' lives, shared about mental health, launched a business, hosted a podcast, written a book, and so much more. Stop playing God. We already have an awesome God.

Trust His plans; forget yours. After all, His plans promise prosperity and protection while offering hope and a future (Jeremiah 29:11).

What plans can you surrender to God today?

_____

_____

_____

_____

_____

_____

_____

_____

_____

_____

_____

_____

_____

_____

_____

_____

_____

_____

_____

_____

DAY FOUR

"Don't store up treasures here on earth, where moths eat them and rust destroys them, and where thieves break in and steal. Store your treasures in heaven, where moths and rust cannot destroy, and thieves do not break in and steal"
(Matthew 6:19–20).

One of my friends calls me "Big Deal Dobbs." He calls me that even when I don't see it. Whether I'm an athlete or a sideline reporter, when I'm leading or following, and even when I was injured and had everything ripped from me. "Big Deal Dobbs" no matter what.

You are a big deal, too. And not because of anything you've done but because of everything God has done for you. Remember, your identity is rooted in Jesus Christ, and you are a big deal because the God of the universe created you, formed you, knit you together, knew you, chose you, set you apart, set plans for you, and sent His Son to die on the cross for you—all before you achieved anything (Titus 3:3–6).

When I suffered my career-ending injury and lost everything in the blink of an eye with one bad block move, I quickly realized the only thing that deserved boasting in my life was Jesus Christ. I couldn't place my identity in worldly accomplishments.

Pressure is released when you play where your feet are because your confidence no longer needs to come from you. Thank God for that. "We are confident of all this because of our great trust in God through Christ. It is not that we think we are qualified to do anything on our own. Our qualification comes from God" (2 Corinthians 3:4-5).

In what are you currently rooting your identity? How can you be sure your identity is rooted in Christ?

.

_____

_____

_____

_____

_____

_____

_____

_____

_____

_____

_____

_____

_____

_____

_____

_____

_____

_____

_____

_____

_____

_____

DAY FIVE

One day Jesus came from Nazareth in Galilee, and John baptized him in the Jordan River. As Jesus came up out of the water, he saw the heavens splitting apart and the Holy Spirit descending on him like a dove. And a voice from heaven said, "You are my dearly loved Son, and you bring me great joy"
(Mark 1:9–11).

Notice something in this scripture. These are the words God spoke when Jesus committed His life to the Lord—not when He entered His ministry. He had yet to perform one single miracle, heal one blind eye, raise one dead man, or feed one crowd with a few fish. He simply committed.

God is not asking for perfection. He is not picking apart your past. When God formed you in your mother's womb, He saw your life in full. He saw the pain, the hurt, the mistakes, the moments you might regret. Still, He said, "That is a life worth creating." God saw how *you* specifically would play where your feet are, exactly where you are—not where you wish you were. You are a life needed on this earth, and your story was made to be told.

Paul and David wrote some of my favorite Bible verses. Before finding Christ, Paul killed Christians. David committed adultery and then killed his mistress's husband. These two men were anything but perfect. But I think that's how they understood how good God was. God was willing to love and use them, despite their sins. He erased their shame and gave them eternal life—the same as He will do for you. Remember, God sent His Son to die on the cross for you before you did anything—good or bad. God loves you as you are and where you are. He just wants you to buy in. He wants you to commit. Give Him your life and see the wonders He works through it.

What area of your life can you surrender today? What sin have you not confessed? How can you take a step toward committing to God today?

_____

_____

_____

_____

_____

_____

_____

_____

_____

_____

_____

_____

_____

_____

_____

_____

_____

_____

_____

_____

_____

DAY SIX

Work willingly at whatever you do, as though you were
working for the Lord rather than for people
(Colossians 3:23).

Every coach in college athletics has their own saying, tagline, or marketing motto. When Hugh Freeze was hired as the head football coach at Auburn University, it was all about the "Freeze Warning on the Plains." In Manny Diaz's first year at the University of Miami, the tagline was "The New Miami."

When Coach Mario Cristobal took the reins from Diaz, there was no marketing motto, but he did have one philosophy he applied to his entire football program: "How you do anything is how you do everything." He said these words in press conferences, team meetings, and casual conversations, and I loved it. I believed it. I modeled it. After all, playing where your feet are emphasizes the same thing—doing your best and being your best, no matter what, no matter where. Everything is intentional. Every day is impactful.

At ten years old, during my first private training session with one of the top coaches at my volleyball club, I hustled even when shagging balls. When I first sprinted after a ball, the coach, confused, asked, "Where are you going?" I paused, pointed to the spare ball, and told him I was shagging.

How I did anything was how I did everything. Even picking up a ball after play, I did so to the best of my ability, whether it seemed normal to onlookers or not. But this approach isn't original to me or to Coach Cristobal but to Colossians. Paul teaches us that whatever we do—anything and everything—we are to do it with all our heart and with the mindset that it is for God. Everything with excellence.

What is one area of your life in which you are lacking excellence? Pray to God today to give you the strength and focus to heighten your hustle.

_____

_____

_____

_____

_____

_____

_____

_____

_____

_____

_____

_____

_____

_____

_____

_____

_____

_____

_____

_____

DAY SEVEN

*"The thief's purpose is to steal and kill and destroy. My
purpose is to give them a rich and satisfying life"*
(John 10:10).

People often ask me, "What *don't* you do?" Typically, I give
the same response, shrugging off such a busy life with a smile
and a "Good question!" But I'll be honest with you. It takes
continuous and endless sacrifice, an unyielding work ethic,
motivation, perseverance, and, for the longest time, an
overwhelming amount of stress and anxiety.

I was once the queen of "fake it 'til you make it." The
phrase embodies an unyielding willingness to reach for a
goal, but, for many years, I took this too far. You don't want
to fake your way through life. Maybe fake it for a moment
until you find your footing in a new role, then find the help
and strength to improve mentally, physically, and spiritually
so that you no longer have to.

The quote "It's okay to not be okay" is often thrown
around. I agree; it *is* okay to not be okay. But let's not stay
there. It's *play* where your feet are, not *stay* where your feet
are. Let's get back to being okay. Let's not just be okay, let's
be better. Don't live a fake life. Live a full life.

The first step in playing where your feet are is understanding where your feet actually are. Forget about faking it. What position are you really in physically, mentally, emotionally, and spiritually? Whatever the answer, good or bad, take that and move forward.

_____

_____

_____

_____

_____

_____

_____

_____

_____

_____

_____

_____

_____

_____

_____

_____

_____

_____

_____

_____

_____

DAY EIGHT

"Of all the commandments, which is the most important?"
Jesus replied, "The most important commandment is this:
'Listen, O Israel! The Lord our God is the one and only Lord.
And you must love the Lord your God with all your heart, all
your soul, all your mind, and all your strength.' The second is
equally important: 'Love your neighbor as yourself.' No other
commandment is greater than these"
(Mark 12:28–31).

Loving your neighbor as yourself can be tough if you don't
already love yourself.

When I medically retired, I endured six months with
zero athletic activity. The closest I came to running was
walking . . . one to two miles per hour on a treadmill—about
as far from running as possible without being stationary.
Standing still just barely has it beat.

As I healed and regained strength, I felt pathetic.
Where I once bench-pressed seventy-pound dumbbells, I now
struggled with fifteen-pounders. The negative self-talk that
clouded my mind was never-ending. And it was real. So real
that during a workout one day, I dropped to my knees and
repeated, "Shut up. Shut up. Shut up." From then on, I
decided to face the truth—I was, in fact, weak—and take
action without believing self-condemning lies. I set realistic
goals. Then, I played where my feet were, first by
acknowledging where my feet were, whether I liked it or not.

Negative thoughts often will try to enter your mind to
ruin your day. Don't beat yourself up for having bad thoughts.
Simply beat the bad thoughts. John 10:4–5 explains that
sheep listen to their shepherd but run from strangers' voices.

You have the power to choose what you listen to. Listen to the truth. Run from anything else.

What lies are you currently believing? Acknowledge them, declare them as lies, and replace them with God's truth.

_____

_____

_____

_____

_____

_____

_____

_____

_____

_____

_____

_____

_____

_____

_____

_____

_____

_____

_____

_____

_____

_____

_____

DAY NINE

"You will never defeat your enemies until you remove these things from among you" (Joshua 7:13).

In my time as a college athlete, game days were always the best. This was true for many reasons: the competition, the fans, the family, the uniforms, and the hype. But if I'm honest, another reason is because they were the easiest. So, naturally, they were the days I felt at my best. The experience was exhilarating.

My former club coach, Suzanne Fitzgerald, always told my team that practice is made to be hard so that the matches are easy. During practices, we'd train hard, lift extra, and grow under burden. Then, when game day arrived, when the time came for us to give our best, we'd release the burden. We'd let go of the ropes holding us back. We weren't playing with weighted vests. We were no longer restricted, we were free.

The same goes for the game of life. We can't be burdened by extra material that weighs us down and trips us up. Weight serves a purpose for a season, but we don't need it forever. We train with extra weight, but we never play with extra weight.

You won't achieve your greatest outcome by overwhelming yourself. Trials bring strength, but your cares must be cast when it's go-time. To move forward, you must let go of what's holding you back. To live in the light, first, lighten your load.

What's holding you back? What is preventing you from playing? What do you need to let go of?

_____

_____

_____

_____

_____

_____

_____

_____

_____

_____

_____

_____

_____

_____

_____

_____

_____

_____

_____

_____

_____

DAY TEN

Oh, don't worry; we wouldn't dare say that we are as wonderful as these other men who tell you how important they are! But they are only comparing themselves with each other, using themselves as the standard of measurement. How ignorant! (2 Corinthians 10:12).

In just one year of my career, I transitioned between starting, battling injury, being benched, switching positions, and medically retiring. I saw my body changing: gaining muscle, maintaining muscle, losing muscle, rebuilding muscle, and managing fat. I became insecure, obsessed with calories. I desperately wanted to be thin. I thought, "When I retire, I'll lose my bulky muscles and my legs will be skinnier. I'll be so thin!"

Plot twist: I lost all my muscle but *kept* the bulkiness. I struggled not only with comparing myself to others but also to my former, game-ready self. I had to remind myself that my body was unique to me and only me, and, frankly, I should be thankful it had withstood everything it had in the past year. I mean, come on. Are you kidding me? My body is incredible, and so is yours!

And not just your body either. Your creativity, your abilities, your unique set of characteristics—everything about you is distinctive to you and only you. You are your greatest asset. Your most marketable quality is that there is not a single person on this planet the same as you.

Comparison is an exhausting cycle of doom. Why waste time comparing yourself with others? We can be much more productive with our energy.

In what ways are you currently struggling with comparison? Empower yourself by stating what you are grateful for in the same area. Ask God for confidence to walk in who He made you to be.

_____

_____

_____

_____

_____

_____

_____

_____

_____

_____

_____

_____

_____

_____

_____

_____

_____

_____

_____

_____

_____

DAY ELEVEN

The one thing I ask of the Lord—the thing I seek most—is to live in the house of the Lord all the days of my life, delighting in the Lord's perfections and meditating in his Temple (Psalm 27:4).

How much do you relate to that verse? Is He the only thing you ask for, the only thing you seek? No? If we're being honest, that's not always my priority either. But it should be.

Truthfully, I am a recovering workaholic who relapses often. I am obsessed with my daily to-do list, which encourages more stress than productivity. Today I have thirty-two tasks to be completed after my full-time job. Estimating each task to take ten minutes translates to three hundred and twenty minutes of work—roughly five and a half hours! If I were to grind immediately when I get home, I would wrap up at midnight. Add a meal and a workout, and we are looking toward a bedtime of approximately two a.m. That is not sustainable, nor is it biblical.

British philosopher Alan Watts said, "Stop measuring days by degree of productivity and start experiencing them by degree of presence."[1] May I suggest squeezing in the word "God's" before "presence"? A day's success should not be measured by how many items on your to-do list were checked off but by how connected you were to Christ.

Even from a Christian's perspective, don't get so caught up in the kingdom that you forget the King. Yes, go to church, lead a small group, attend conferences, and more, but don't forget about your alone time with God. That's the priority.

My roommate, Kay, says she can sit in silence with the people she feels closest to. There doesn't have to be a party, dinner, movie, music, anything. She finds complete comfort in the silence. Being still while feeling safe is special. That's what God craves with you.

How can you dwell in God's presence today?

_____

_____

_____

_____

_____

_____

_____

_____

_____

_____

_____

_____

_____

_____

_____

_____

_____

_____

_____

_____

_____

DAY TWELVE

*"And what do you benefit if you gain the whole world but lose
your own soul? Is anything worth more than your soul?"*
(Matthew 16:26).

In 2021 and 2022, my word of the year was "Go." I was to go
with bold and blind faith. If afraid, I would be all in. If
frightened, I would continue, full speed ahead.

Striving for an extended season paid off but wasn't
sustainable in the long term. I was less dependent on God and
more ignorantly dependent on myself. I kept pushing and
pushing and pushing, depleting my energy. On the outside, on
my resume, on my social media, I was gaining the world . . .
all while losing my soul. Exhausted and drained of joy, I
finally paused. I celebrated the two years of intense efforts
and then altered my mindset for 2023 shifting from "go" to
"let go."

To strive less and trust God more, I said, "If God's not
in it, I don't want it. If He's in it, He'll bring it to me. If He's
not bringing anything at the current moment, I'll steward
what He's already brought because that, in and of itself, is
already an answered prayer." For 365 days, I repeated that
prayer. Now, I let go of the things that pass me by, knowing
they are not for me nor are they of God. If I'm walking with
God and in His will, I won't miss what He has uniquely for
me. It took twenty-five years, but I now know the meaning of
"laughing without fear of the future," as mentioned in
Proverbs 31.

Anything good is of God. Gaining the world is not. Where can you give up the world and give in to God today?

_____

_____

_____

_____

_____

_____

_____

_____

_____

_____

_____

_____

_____

_____

_____

_____

_____

_____

_____

_____

_____

_____

DAY THIRTEEN

Always be joyful. Never stop praying. Be thankful in all circumstances, for this is God's will for you who belong to Christ Jesus (1 Thessalonians 5:16–18).

God's will—a phrase you've probably heard before. Maybe you have prayed that God's will would be done. Maybe you've wondered what is God's will for your life: whether to take this job, transfer to this college, date this person, or live in this city.

We know from 1 Kings 8:58 that we are to obey God's will, and Romans 12:2 says God's will is "good and pleasing and perfect." But what is God's will? How nice would it be to know God's plan for your life!

Well, can I surprise you today? God spells it out for us in the Bible. At the end of "Paul's Final Advice" in 1 Thessalonians 5:16–18, Paul points us to this: "Always be joyful. Never stop praying. Be thankful in all circumstances, for this is God's will for you who belong to Christ Jesus."

That's it! That is what you are to do! Everything else is just a byproduct. Study this or that major? Flip a coin, choose tails, then . . . always be joyful, never stop praying, and be thankful in all circumstances. Pursue this or that career? Do what makes you happy, then . . . always be joyful, never stop praying, and be thankful in all circumstances. Do whatever you want, following God's Word, then . . . always be joyful, never stop praying, and be thankful in all circumstances.

Don't complicate the Christian life when God simply wants your heart. Whichever route you take, play where your feet are. Do your best and be your best, no matter what and no matter where. Pour into that position, and if God moves you elsewhere, follow Him.

How can you be more joyful? What prayer is currently placed on your heart? What is something for which you are thankful?

_____

_____

_____

_____

_____

_____

_____

_____

_____

_____

_____

_____

_____

_____

_____

_____

_____

_____

DAY FOURTEEN

"For I know the plans I have for you," says the Lord. "They are plans for good and not for disaster, to give you a future and a hope" (Jeremiah 29:11).

God's will for your life is that you would be joyful, pray, and give thanks.

According to the CDC Foundation, a will is "a legal document that describes how you would like your property and other assets to be distributed after your death."[1] God's will details your inheritance. It includes promises that give peace. In Jeremiah 29:11, God promises protection, prosperity, hope, and a future. He doesn't provide day-to-day details, but these promises bring peace. God has a plan. He does for me. He does for you. He did for Joseph, too!

His story goes like this: Joseph is sold into slavery by his jealous brothers. From slavery, he's wrongly accused and sent to prison. Some time later, Pharaoh gets mad at two of his officials and demotes them to prison. Joseph has a special gift of interpreting dreams, and these officials have dreams with no one to interpret them. Joseph interprets, and in return, one of the officials says (in my translation): "Dude! I got you! Once I'm out, I'll tell everyone about you! I'll get you out of here!"

Upon release, the official completely forgets about Joseph. Two years later, Pharaoh is also having dreams no one can interpret. The official, standing nearby says, "Wait! Y'all, I know a guy!" Finally, at the right place, at the right time, Joseph comes into the conversation. He is released from prison, interprets the dreams perfectly, is praised, and placed in authority. There was still protection. There was still prosperity. From prison to the palace, Joseph became ruler of

Egypt. Not his plan, not his timing. Not his desire, not his wish. Not his will. God's.

Where are you struggling to trust God's will in your life? Pray for trust in God, full of peace, through the promises of protection, prosperity, hope, and a future.

THE PRAYER JOURNAL

DAY FIFTEEN

"Take it, my lord the king, and use it as you wish," Araunah said to David. "Here are oxen for the burnt offering, and you can use the threshing boards and ox yokes for wood to build a fire on the altar. I will give it all to you, Your Majesty, and may the Lord your God accept your sacrifice." But the king replied to Araunah, "No, I insist on buying it, for I will not present burnt offerings to the Lord my God that have cost me nothing" (2 Samuel 24:22–24).

Everything good in my life has been preceded by something difficult. Earning a full scholarship to play volleyball at the University of Miami required eight years of club volleyball that pushed me past my physical and mental limits. Building a business came after long strategic meetings and tireless work. Progressing in my career can be credited to getting out of bed and grinding every day, finding stepping stone after stepping stone.

Nothing good ever comes easy. It takes work and preparation. Discipline and dedication. Hustle and hard work. It takes struggle to gain strength. It takes sacrifice to be successful. It takes sacrifice to grow your spirit, too. Sacrifice for God in the same way that you sacrifice for your work, career, sport, social life, spouse, kids, and passion projects. If you give it up for them, you should do the same for God.

The result of sacrificing something of significance was an answered prayer for David (2 Samuel 24:25). It could be the same for you. Sow a seed. Start a fast. Invest in prayer like never before. We don't put a price on our faith, we put priority on it. What you give up will be paid back a hundredfold. This season is intentional, so be intentional in it.

God is an Ephesians 3:20 God who will do more than you could ever ask for or imagine. He is the God of more and will give you more. Prioritize God and believe in His abilities. Don't limit Him by giving less.

What if God is asking for more of you today? What areas of your life do you need to sacrifice? Is it your time, your tithes, your trust?

_____

_____

_____

_____

_____

_____

_____

_____

_____

_____

_____

_____

_____

_____

_____

_____

_____

_____

DAY SIXTEEN

"Be still, and know that I am God!" (Psalm 46:10).

My sister, Kelsey, continuously repeats to me the phrase, "Sharpen the saw."

Imagine you have a saw. You work daily with your saw, but over time, it becomes dull. An unsharpened saw delays progress. It becomes more beneficial to leave your project entirely and spend time sharpening your saw to regain the ability to work efficiently. Why work harder when you can work smarter? Why exhaust yourself with a dull saw?

We are not made to live life exhausted. We are made to live life abundantly, to live life to the fullest, and to live a life full of living. In John 10:10, Jesus says, "The thief's purpose is to steal and kill and destroy. My purpose is to give them a rich and satisfying life." For most of my life, striving for success meant that being burnt out was my baseline. Over time, I realized that life is a marathon, not a sprint. You can't spend a hundred years on this earth sprinting. And how can you stop to smell the roses if you're speeding past them all? Work hard and work intently, yes. However, know that God —not you—is the God of the harvest. You may water the crop, but He grows it. God produces fruitfulness, opens doors, and brings scholarships, opportunities, promotions, and more.

When you think about it, most things in our life are outside our control, but God commands us in Psalm 46:10 to "be still and know that I am God." Being still is the step before reflecting on the fact that He is God. Be still. Pause. Take a breath, take a moment, and know that He is God over all; He is in control.

Look ahead to your schedule this week. Where can you pause to sharpen your saw?

DAY SEVENTEEN

Then the angel spoke to the women. "Don't be afraid!" he
said. "I know you are looking for Jesus, who was crucified.
He isn't here! He is risen from the dead, just as he said would
happen. Come, see where his body was lying. And now, go
quickly and tell his disciples that he has risen from the dead,
and he is going ahead of you to Galilee. You will see him
there. Remember what I have told you." The women ran
quickly from the tomb. They were very frightened but also
filled with great joy, and they rushed to give the disciples
the angel's message (Matthew 28:5–8).

We have discussed the root of playing where your feet are,
the identity you have in Christ, and how you must let go and
trust God to move forward. Now, you need to step out.

I specifically say *play* where your feet are, not *be*
where your feet are. Who wants to just be anyway? I want to
play. I want to utilize the position I'm in. I want to enjoy,
thrive, learn, improve, compete, challenge myself, and
change. Movement is a change in position, and change is vital
for victory. You can't grow if you don't go.

While pursuing my master's in journalism at UM, I
took Michelle Kaufman's Sports Reporting class. The
legendary sportswriter has attended and reported on over a
dozen Olympics and many World Cups. In her class, I
covered all South Florida sports teams and interviewed
professional players of different sports, genders, ages, and
nationalities. Still, out of all the journalistic skills I learned,
my biggest takeaway from her was this: "Life begins at the
end of your comfort zone."

She was right. We can't live a life full of living if we
are too scared to live life. Period. In Matthew 28:9, when

Martha and Mary saw that Jesus's body was gone from the tomb, they knew they needed to run and tell all. They were frightened but ran full speed. Afraid, but all in. We must do the same.

How can you step out of your comfort zone today?

_____

_____

_____

_____

_____

_____

_____

_____

_____

_____

_____

_____

_____

_____

_____

_____

_____

_____

_____

DAY EIGHTEEN

But Jesus replied, "My Father is always working, and so am I" (John 5:17).

When I made my NFL TV debut as guest commentator, I knew the weight it held in my career. I prioritized preparation and reached out to mentors in the field for advice. Eric Mac Lain of the ACC Network told me to know the key stats and base everything on them because the stats don't lie.

The stats don't lie. Our confidence is in God. Why? Because the stats don't lie. Look at what He's done! There are more than a hundred miracles recorded in the Bible—Creation, a donkey speaking, Moses's rod becoming a snake, the Red Sea splitting, water bursting from a rock, Jericho's walls falling, the dead raised to life, three men surviving the fiery furnace, Daniel surviving the lion's den, Jonah surviving the fish's belly, water turned to wine, countless healings, demons removed, a few fish feeding five thousand, Jesus calming the storm and walking on water, and Christ crucified, raised to life after three days, then making numerous appearances.

I'm sorry, but who am I to deny what the Lord can do? The stats don't lie. He has done it before, and He will do it again. Even after Christ's ascension into heaven, the miracles continued. How? Because the power is not only in the person of Jesus Christ but also in the presence of the Holy Spirit.

Even when we have no sight of Christ, we still have no fright. The fact is, I have faith because my Lord is Lord above all. My strength comes from knowing that. I don't have to know the script because I know the director. I don't question the chef at the restaurant, the designer of my clothes, the engineer of the rollercoaster, or the pilot of the plane. I've seen the stats. I've seen it done before. It will be done again.

Reference three times God has come through for you. Ask God to help you remember His faithfulness and His statistics when life gets tough.

_____

_____

_____

_____

_____

_____

_____

_____

_____

_____

_____

_____

_____

_____

_____

_____

_____

_____

_____

DAY NINETEEN

*"Didn't I tell you that you would see God's glory
if you believe?"* (John 11:40).

The Miami Hurricanes baseball team has been nicknamed the "Cardiac Canes." They earned the title because of their frequency of walk-off runs and electric wins. The Canes coming back has become an identity and part of the "Mark Light Magic" that beams in the ballpark.

In March of 2024, the Canes completed their biggest comeback since 1992. After trailing by nine, they topped the thirteenth-ranked Virginia Cavaliers, winning 16–12. Emotions ran high, but not just because of the comeback. The player with the walk-off grand slam was Blake Cyr. Cyr was a standout stud as a freshman, but his sophomore year began quite differently. A week into the season, his father passed away. Cyr took time off, and in his first performance back, hit this walk-off grand slam. When the ball left the bat, Cyr pointed to heaven multiple times with all his might as he rounded the bases. In his post-game interview, an understandably emotional Cyr gave glory to God and sent love to his earthly father above. It will forever mark my career as one of the most touching moments I've reported.

I often warn fans not to leave the game early if they want to see the Canes in their full glory. The game is never finished until the final out, and more than likely, the result will be more than you could ever imagine.

Life with Christ is the same. You can't quit. You can't leave early. God is the King of plot twists and happy endings. You have to watch to the end. Finishing allows you to see promises and prophecies come to fruition. Finishing is fully worth the wait. Keep the faith. Keep believing. The comeback creates an even better testimony.

In what area of your life have you walked away from belief? Renew your belief today. Get back in the game. Watch the prophecy come to fruition.

_____

_____

_____

_____

_____

_____

_____

_____

_____

_____

_____

_____

_____

_____

_____

_____

_____

_____

_____

DAY TWENTY

Victory depends on having many advisers
(Proverbs 24:6).

Every page of this book aims to prepare you to play where your feet are. To do so well, you must have mentorship. Any good player has a good coach. Any good team has a good leader. Any good business has a good CEO.

Growing up playing at the top club volleyball program in the nation, I had fantastic teachers. I was trained by the best at the University of Miami. Now that my athletic career is over, the coaching doesn't end. I might be an adult, but there is much room to grow. I am forever seeking mentorship in my career field, personal life, spiritual walk, and more. I have trusted advisers who guide, push, challenge, and check me.

Note: Proverbs doesn't say, "Victory depends on having many friends." We will address friends shortly; let's first focus on advisers. Advisers speak life into you and pray over you. They are experts in their fields and examples to follow. You should aim to model them in their work, faith, family, or lifestyle.

Who do you consider your mentor and why? If you do not have a mentor, who will you ask? Find a mentor living a life similar to your aspirations—examine their work/life balance, marriage, parenting, etc.

DAY TWENTY-ONE

As iron sharpens iron, so a friend sharpens a friend
(Proverbs 27:17).

I believe the best way to better ourselves is to hang out with better people.

Working to improve academic programs at Harvard University, Professor Richard Elmore said, "Isolation is the enemy of improvement."[1] Sounds to me like Elmore thinks we cannot better ourselves without others surrounding us, in our corner, on our team. We cannot get better when we are apart. *Isolation is the enemy of improvement.*

The Bible is seemingly on the same page as Elmore. In Mark 2, a paralyzed man is surrounded by healthy friends who go above and beyond to break barriers and extend to extreme heights for him . . . literally. His friends climb the roof of a home where Jesus is, dig a hole through this roof, and lower their friend inside, skipping the crowds to get him to his Savior. Because of their faith and pursuit of God, Jesus heals their friend.

Your friends have a great impact on you. If chosen incorrectly, they will allow you to *stay* where your feet are. But if chosen correctly? They will push you to play where your feet are. With good friends and great faith, the opportunities for God to work are truly endless.

Consider your five closest friends. Are you surrounding yourself with strong friends who can launch you to new levels and put you in the presence of Christ?

_____

_____

_____

_____

_____

_____

_____

_____

_____

_____

_____

_____

_____

_____

_____

_____

_____

_____

_____

_____

_____

DAY TWENTY-TWO

"I will lead blind Israel down a new path, guiding them along an unfamiliar way. I will brighten the darkness before them and smooth out the road ahead of them. Yes, I will indeed do these things; I will not forsake them" (Isaiah 42:16).

This verse might have a sense of scare in it, but it is truthfully so comforting when you look more closely.

God never says He will give us sight or steer us away from unfamiliar paths. Jesus made it clear that a Christian's life would not be easy in this world. He knew the disciples would face trials and tribulations. He gave them the Word, and in turn, they were hated by the world. Did He pray that they would be taken out of the world? No. Jesus prayed they would stay in the world but know they are not of it (John 17:14–15). We have purpose in this life, in our position, and where our feet are.

When the path ahead is full of rocks, stumps, and obstacles, I pray and encourage you to keep on keeping on. Keep asking. Keep seeking. Keep knocking. Keep pushing when all odds are stacked against you. Work hard when the haters say you won't make it. Stay the course when you're the only one on it. Keep chasing your dream when your dream is running faster than you. Like in the Christmas movie classic *A Year Without Santa Claus*, just keep putting one foot in front of the other. The way might seem unfamiliar, but God will guide you. Proverbs 3:5–6 encourages us that when we place our trust in Him, He will make our paths straight. Trust Him, and the trail smooths.

What path are you currently walking that seems unfamiliar? Ask God to be your guiding light.

DAY TWENTY-THREE

And now, dear brothers and sisters, one final thing. Fix your thoughts on what is true, and honorable, and right, and pure, and lovely, and admirable. Think about things that are excellent and worthy of praise (Philippians 4:8).

My friend recently moved into a new apartment. She was obsessed, as it boasted great square footage, beautiful floor-to-ceiling windows overlooking the city, amazing flooring, and great amenities in a fabulous location. The place had it all . . . including popcorn ceilings. *Yikes.* Her heart was determined to make her new home aesthetically pleasing, and these popcorn ceilings were quite the distraction. So, we went to work, googling how to remove popcorn ceilings in a rental space. The search, however, proved unsuccessful—it turns out, you can't.

We checked for alternate solutions. Want to know what was recommended? When living in an apartment complex where you can't remodel or remove the popcorn ceilings, bring attention elsewhere. If you can't eliminate the bad, bring attention to the good. New goal: bring attention to the floor!

When tough things happen, be tough. Toughness, as defined by the 2019 Hurricanes volleyball team meant to *skip the junk and make a plan*. Recognize the junk you might be in, the junk where your feet are. There is no need to cry over spilt milk. Focus on the better. Focus on the things listed above in Philippians 4:8 and make a plan to play.

What junk do you need to skip? What plan can you make today—from rekindling a friendship to cleaning up a spill?

_____

_____

_____

_____

_____

_____

_____

_____

_____

_____

_____

_____

_____

_____

_____

_____

_____

_____

_____

_____

_____

DAY TWENTY-FOUR

Be strong, all you people still left in the land. And now get to work, for I am with you, says the LORD of Heaven's Armies (Haggai 2:4).

Caitlin Smith, my strength coach at the University of Miami, was a beast. Sure, she encouraged us to throw some weight around, but she was forever the strongest of all. Nothing fired us up more than when she would send videos in our group chat of her hitting her personal bests. During our workouts, our assistant coach, Jillian Hadder, and director of operations, Natalia "Gaby" Huaroto-Luque, even hopped in to grind with us.

There is always something so empowering about having your leaders grind with you. They're not just yelling at you to do the work. They're doing the work with you.

Haggai 2:4 is a pregame speech I'd be fired up to hear. In this scripture, God tells His people to be strong, assuring them of the strength He knows lies inside. When the going got tough, God used tough love. He didn't sugarcoat the struggle; He reminded them He was with them, by their side through it all. But He called them to action; He called them to go.

Remember that God is with you. God goes before you. He has already walked through those places you have yet to place a foot. He will give you strength and stand by your side. Trust His leadership. Trust His path. Trust His presence.

Where are you lacking strength? Where is fear holding you back?

_____

_____

_____

_____

_____

_____

_____

_____

_____

_____

_____

_____

_____

_____

_____

_____

_____

_____

_____

_____

_____

_____

_____

DAY TWENTY-FIVE

"Well done!" the king exclaimed. "You are a good servant.
You have been faithful with the little I entrusted to you, so you
will be governor of ten cities as your reward" (Luke 19:17).

Before being hired as TV host and producer for *Inside South
Florida*, WSFL Channel 39, I auditioned with the station.
First, I was brought on the show as a guest. Then, I put
together a feature story. I tested in-studio and on-air, and,
later, I appeared as guest commentator for the NFL post-game
show. I guest-hosted the show for a week before receiving the
full-time offer. Each new role brought more responsibility.
Each opportunity led to the next. My three-minute debut
developed into a multi-year contract. Although the first gig
seemed minimal, it was a building block to a career path.
Your opportunities too, both big and small, are the same.

Along with "Play where your feet are," my mom is
known for another piercing phrase: "It's a tryout." Everything
in life, she taught, is a tryout. You never know how one day,
one game, one play, person, interview, or interaction might
change your life. But don't let this truth overwhelm you!
Rather, let it be a reminder to approach everything with
intention.

God looks at what you *can* do, not what you can't do.
He looks to see if you are playing where your feet are.
Working in the now. Staying expectant of the future. He looks
to see what you are doing where you are and with what you
already have.

Luke 19:17 showcases the goal—not to govern ten
cities, but that when we approach God, He would commend
the works we have done, without regard to our money,
residence, resume, Instagram followers, or jeans size.

Zechariah 4:10 says, "Do not despise these small beginnings." If you do much with little, God will reward your little with much. He only needs a little to do a lot and will use mustard-seed-sized faith to move mountains.

Every day is a tryout.

What is one small step of faith you can take today that can propel your relationship with God?

DAY TWENTY-SIX

You will show me the way of life, granting me the joy of your presence and the pleasures of living with you forever
(Psalm 16:11).

The words *can't wait!* are always at the top of my vocabulary. I am constantly planning ahead, looking forward to what's next. During high school, I couldn't wait for college. In college, it was my career. In singleness, a relationship.

But it's worse than that. I often sat in class thinking about what I would eat for dinner; while eating dinner, I thought through the homework I had to do; while working on homework, I planned breakfast; while eating breakfast, I wondered about practice; and at practice, I prepared myself for class. It's no different for me today. If I'm not careful, it can become an exhausting cycle of looking ahead and missing the moment.

Expectancy is not fruitless, but we shouldn't fixate on it. The future is bright, but there is purpose in the present. If nothing else, it is that God is present with you. Don't miss what He has for you today, in this season, exactly where your feet are.

God commands us to be still. Psalms 16:11 says, "Your presence is the fullness of joy." Joy is at its greatest in God's presence. We should find joy in simply sitting with God, resting in our current season, and trusting God's timing. Verse 11 ends with, "at your right hand are pleasures forevermore." If all the pleasures are with God, I want to draw near to Him and stay near Him. God is here. God is now. Stay present with Him. See what He is doing.

Sit in gratitude and reflect upon three ways you see God working in your life.

_____

_____

_____

_____

_____

_____

_____

_____

_____

_____

_____

_____

_____

_____

_____

_____

_____

_____

_____

_____

_____

_____

DAY TWENTY-SEVEN

Then Jesus said, "Come to me, all of you who are weary and carry heavy burdens, and I will give you rest"
(Matthew 11:28).

When facing a decision, my dad often opts to, in his words, "sleep on it." For anything from a job offer to a dinner destination, he will take a nap or sleep through the night before deciding. Time after time, nap after nap, he wakes up with clarity and confidence in a choice. It never fails—a little bit of sleep, and he is suddenly sure of himself . . . and I think there's something to it.

In Matthew 11:28 above, God's solution to weariness and being burdened is rest. Not clarity. Not a relationship. Not a good grade or a new job. Not even an answered prayer. *Rest.*

When the storms raged in Mark 4, the disciples were freaking out while Jesus slept soundly. When I find myself overwhelmed with tasks and to-do's, I am, in reality, neglecting rest. Maybe my prayer should not be for efficiency or the will to exercise supernatural powers of productivity but, rather, to surrender control of my time and tasks and submit to sleep.

The New Living Translation is my favorite translation of Psalm 23:1–2. Why? One key word: *lets.* It says, "He *lets* me rest." This is one of the most convicting lines I have ever read because rest is a gift. It is a privilege. God *lets* you do it. How kind of Him. Find peace in His presence. He wants you to feel refreshed and renewed with strength, but the solution is not to strive so much that you barely survive. It is a mix of focusing on the task while exercising the freedom to release control to Christ.

Let yourself lie down. Let go. Let God. Remember, joy comes in the morning. Sometimes you just need to go to sleep so you can wake up to a fresh kind of joy. Enjoy the gift He freely gives.

If rest is a gift, how often do you accept it? How can you rest today? Can you take ten minutes to read your Bible? Go for a walk? Go to bed by ten? Commit to doing one small act of rest today.

_____

_____

_____

_____

_____

_____

_____

_____

_____

_____

_____

_____

_____

_____

_____

_____

DAY TWENTY-EIGHT

Wait patiently for the Lord. Be brave and courageous. Yes, wait patiently for the Lord (Psalm 27:14).

Waiting is hard . . . *really* hard. But it shouldn't cause weariness. If you are weary, the Bible says in Matthew 11:28 to go to Jesus, and He will give you rest. Rest is a solution for weariness.

Waiting isn't about speeding up the time, it's about resting in it. David's advice? Read that verse above again. Go ahead, I'll wait.

Okay, you've read the verse again? Let's examine. It's like David told you to wait patiently, saw the reaction on your face, the dismissal in your eyes, and said, "No, seriously. That's what I said. You heard me right—or maybe you need to hear me again . . . you have to *wait patiently* for the Lord." I also love how "be brave and courageous" is sandwiched in there as the perfect reminder that patience requires bravery and courage.

We aren't supposed to be weary in the waiting. Sure, it's tough, but you are tough too. You can withstand tough things. As Pastor Mary Alessi of Metro Life Church in Miami says, "The delay is deliberate." There is a reason for the season . . . yes, even slow seasons. God's timing is everything, even when we don't see everything in God's timing. It takes bravery to believe and courage to be confident. Be active while you wait. Play where your feet are.

In what area are you being called to wait? How are you using your wait time? How can you exhibit bravery and courage?

_____

_____

_____

_____

_____

_____

_____

_____

_____

_____

_____

_____

_____

_____

_____

_____

_____

_____

_____

_____

_____

_____

_____

_____

DAY TWENTY-NINE

A woman in the crowd had suffered for twelve years with constant bleeding. She had suffered a great deal from many doctors, and over the years she had spent everything she had to pay them, but she had gotten no better. In fact, she had gotten worse. She had heard about Jesus, so she came up behind him through the crowd and touched his robe. For she thought to herself, "If I can just touch his robe, I will be healed." Immediately the bleeding stopped (Mark 5:25–29).

Whenever I think of a waiting season, I cannot help but think of this woman. Twelve years of suffering. Then, all of a sudden, she changes her life with a quick-twitch reflex to stretch for the cloak of Christ in blind faith that God would heal her if she drew near. Her faith healed her instantly.

It doesn't seem like this woman overthought the situation, considered what others might think about her action, or even hesitated to make the move. She knew God could perform miracles and believed her health could be one of them. Her lifetime of waiting came down to a moment. When given the chance, she did not miss her opportunity. She was prepared.

Be expectant. You never know when your waiting period will be over. You never know when Coach will need you—or for how long. God knows the desires of your heart, and He will do exceedingly and abundantly more than you can ever ask for or imagine (Ephesians 3:20). Train and prepare so that when you are called, you can perform.

You never know when God will call. Your moment is coming, but it must be preceded by preparation. God doesn't always place things in your lap, but He does put things in your reach. Do the work and extend your arm. Draw near to God. Stretch to seek Him, whatever it takes.

Where can you prepare today to be ready for tomorrow?

DAY THIRTY

Then Jesus asked them, "Would anyone light a lamp and then put it under a basket or under a bed? Of course not! A lamp is placed on a stand, where its light will shine" (Mark 4:21).

In the summer of 2020, amidst the coronavirus pandemic, I was tasked with independent study to finish incomplete courses from the prior semester during my last and most severe concussion. Of those courses, meteorology consumed most of my time . . . and created most of my stress!

One beautiful, cloud-free summer day, while trapped inside studying severe weather and forecasting methods, I repeatedly read in my science book that no matter how good the technology becomes at telling us about approaching storms, warnings will not be effective unless we take note, absorb the information, and take action. If we don't heed the warnings, they will be useless, and lives may be lost. After becoming frustrated with my studies, I paused to hop off my bitter bus—those forecasts were similar to God's Word! The Bible is the instruction manual of life; it is our playbook. But what good is a playbook if we do not execute the plays? If we don't take note, absorb the information, and take action, the Word may become pointless to us, and—most significantly—*eternal* lives may be lost.

James 4:17 says, "Remember, it is a sin to know what you ought to do and then not do it." Our charge in life is to live a life full of living, not to *plan* a life full of living. It is playing where our feet are in any and all circumstances. Playing is an action. Don't hide the truth of the Gospel. Don't hide your light. Heed the warnings. Spread the word. This isn't about earthly storms; this is about eternal salvation.

Are you taking up space or taking advantage? Who in your life has yet to see the Light of Christ shining from you? Where can you make a more intentional impact?

_____

_____

_____

_____

_____

_____

_____

_____

_____

_____

_____

_____

_____

_____

_____

_____

_____

_____

_____

_____

DAY THIRTY-ONE

This is the day the Lord has made. We will rejoice and be glad in it (Psalm 118:24).

My roommate, Kay, and I joke that playing *We're Not Really Strangers* is an initiation into our household. This card game focuses on perception, connection, and reflection. It turns strangers into family in only a few minutes. Each card has questions to dive deeper into the way one thinks. One question reads, "What feeling do you miss?" Kay always answers, "Childhood."

It makes me think of the word "play" and what it means to me—the intensity, the work, the hustle. However, I often need a reminder of what "play" first meant—friends, recess, dodgeball, Barbie dolls, joy, laughter, freedom . . . weightless shoulders. But these don't have to be feelings of the past. "Play" is something we can recreate today through sport, community, friendship, hobbies, and, ultimately, Christ.

"Play where your feet are" is my mother's daily encouragement to find purpose in every position. I have been blessed with two amazing parents. My dad always inserted an important reminder at the end of each motivational moment. Peptalks always ended with ". . . and have fun!" An important reminder that life should be fun—even while working. There is joy in playing. There is joy in playing where your feet are.

Play should be interchangeable with joy. Play should be a priority. It is our strength in life. Nehemiah 8:10 says, "The joy of the Lord is your strength!" Look to the Lord when you're looking for joy. Run after today.

Day 1 of this journal restarts after today's message. I encourage you to read through the daily devotions again. Review your notes, dig deeper, and watch your progression.

Be deliberate in finding joy by committing to a life full of living. Play where your feet are.

In what ways will you pursue joy today and play where your feet are?

_____

_____

_____

_____

_____

_____

_____

_____

_____

_____

_____

_____

_____

_____

_____

_____

_____

_____

_____

ADDITIONAL REFLECTIONS

ADDITIONAL REFLECTIONS

_____

_____

_____

_____

_____

_____

_____

_____

_____

_____

_____

_____

_____

_____

_____

_____

_____

_____

_____

_____

_____

NOTES

DAY ELEVEN

[1] Alan Watts, British philosopher, (January 6, 1915–November 16, 1973).

DAY FOURTEEN

[1] "What Is a Will?" *CDC Foundation,* www.cdcfoundation.org/give/will#:~:text=A%20will%2C%20or%20a%20last,be%20distributed%20after%20your%20death. Accessed 15 Jan. 2024.

DAY TWENTY-ONE

[1] Richard F. Elmore, "Building a New Structure for School Leadership," *American Educator* (Winter 1999-2000), American Federation of Teachers, https://www.aft.org/periodical/american-educator/winter-1999-2000.

ABOUT THE AUTHOR

Cameron Dobbs is a light. Her story of triumph over tragedy is a call to action, inspiring each to find our purpose, whatever the position. Her lessons will ignite your soul and help you discover joy, even during the waiting seasons.

Cameron grew up in a close-knit, Christ-following, and high-achieving family in the suburbs of Atlanta, Georgia. She played NCAA Division I volleyball for the University of Miami until a career-ending injury led to a medical disqualification during her junior season. After a time spent mourning the loss of her dreams and suffering the effects of the injury, she began to turn things around, taking on a new role as the team's student assistant coach and finishing her bachelor's degree in broadcast journalism and master's degree in journalism, both summa cum laude.

Cameron has since spent many hours as a sports reporter, event host, producer, and an on-air personality for The U, ACC Network, Stadium, WSFL Channel 39, Florida Panthers, and others. She was featured as a "Difference Maker" on CNN, and HLN for her work with Operation Christmas Child. She was inducted into the prestigious Iron Arrow Society and "30 Under 30" recognizing outstanding alumni for the University of Miami. She co-owns PWYFA Play Where Your Feet Are™ with her mother and travels the country speaking to universities, schools, faith-based organizations, athletes, and audiences of all ages, fulfilling her passion to help others live a life full of living. Cameron coaches volleyball clinics and hosts the *PWYFA Play Where Your Feet Are*™ podcast, retreats, webinars, and more.

We invite you to live and rep the PWYFA Play Where Your Feet Are™ brand, purchase your copy of her first book, and engage with us. Merchandise can be shipped anywhere in the USA and found on the PWYFA Play Where Your Feet Are™ website. Learn more about PWYFA Play Where Your Feet Are™ by inviting Cameron to an event, booking her for an experience, or simply reaching out to be friends. She loves connecting with others, so send her a message!

Email: playwhereyourfeetare@gmail.com
Website: playwhereyourfeetare.com
Facebook: Play Where Your Feet Are
Instagram: @playwhereyourfeetare+@cam.dobbs

Made in the USA
Columbia, SC
20 April 2025

edc4635f-33b0-4b82-b850-1bc3d73f9040R01